# A JOURNEY OF SELF DISCOVERY

# A JOURNEY OF SELF DISCOVERY

## My Short Story

MARY CLUCKIE

*Paul Colquhoun, Belinda Hoole*

Mary Cluckie

# CONTENTS

~ 1 ~

THE SECOND WORLD WAR

1

~ 2 ~

BATTLE OF BRITAIN

4

~ 3 ~

THE BOMBING OF LONDON – THE BLITZ

7

~ 4 ~

CREATE YOUR DESTINY

28

~ 1 ~

# THE SECOND WORLD WAR

The months after the war started were pretty quiet, but not so in Germany. Adolf Hitler

Invaded Poland on the 1st of September, he thought he was invincible as the next country was

France. The Jews had no part in this evil Dictator's plans, they had to be exterminated. So began the moving of the Jews to camps which came to be known as the horrific holocaust. Hitler looked upon himself as becoming the most powerful being on this earth. What was known as the Third Reich came to be Hitler's sacred ground, the military bowed down to him and treated him like a pagan God.

As soon as the war started food was rationed in England. We were issued with ration books. Meat was in short supply before long and rabbit stew was a popular pot on the stove! We were allowed 2 rashers of bacon each per week as pork was scarce, chickens were also few and far between, we were issued with dried eggs which were not very appetising. We were allowed one roast per week, mainly roast lamb, this became less as time went on as sheep began to disappear from the fields.

When we did have a roast my mother would make sure there was plenty of dripping as this tasted better than the margarine we were issued. Each member of the family received 2 ounces of butter per week, this did not go very far, especially on toast for breakfast. That is when the dripping usually

took the place of butter.

## ~ 2 ~

# BATTLE OF BRITAIN

10th July 1940 - 31st October 1940

The Battle of Britain was an aerial battle between the German fighter planes (Messerschmitts) and the Royal Air Force, Fighter Command. It took place mainly over South England. As I lived in Southeast England, I could watch the "dogfights" overhead, I admit pretty scary! The 15th of September was the turning point in the Battle of Britain..... 56 German fighter planes were shot down, this one day tally convinced Adolf Hitler that not only could the Luftwaffe gain aerial superiority over England, but also the English Channel. This was the first major defeat for the Germans in WW11.

The British victory prevented Operation Sea Lion, a planned German airborne and amphibious invasion of Britain from going ahead. As the first of Hitler's military forces defeat in WW11, this was an important factor in boosting the morale of both the British public and the military. Hitler was determined he was going to hang onto the belief that he was invincible, he turned his eyes towards Russia. He saw it could be a threat to his Balkan oil supply, at least he imagined this was possible, so he put into action

Nazi Germany's ideological goal of conquering the Western Soviet Union with the idea of repopulating it with Germans.

~ 3 ~

# THE BOMBING OF LONDON – THE BLITZ

7th September 1940 - 11th May 1941

The main targets at first were the London Docks, with the idea of stopping merchant ships from coming into port. Liverpool was and still is a large dock area in London surrounded by terrace houses. For 3 consecutive nights this area was bombed causing so much destruction to the docks and houses plus terrible losses of lives.

The German bombers then made Central London the target for many nights with again shocking losses of lives. Then the outlying suburbs began to get the onslaught of the bombing.

The 9th of November has and always will stand out in my memory, this was the night our suburb "copped it". My father had previously installed a corrugated steel air raid shelter in our lounge, not exactly adding to the décor of the room! However, we did not have to go out into the street to a public air raid shelter.

There were 5 of us living in the house….. mother, father, my sister and myself, plus my grandfather who was living with us at the time. We had a reservoir running through the outskirts of our suburb which was and still is the Sunbury-on-Thames. On this particular night the Germans made the reservoir their target. We used to say "What is going to be the target for tonight!?" This particular night the air raid siren had sounded but it was still pretty quiet, so my mother ventured out of the shelter into the kitchen, where she always made my grandfather hot bread and milk before he went to bed (I know it sounds revolting!). In those days we did not have electric jugs or microwave ovens. Mother lit the gas stove and was heating the milk on the stove, when the sound of German bombers were heard. She put the gas out and hurried back to the shelter. The next thing we heard was an explosion not so very far away, and then all went quiet, so my father ventured out into the street, where he was met by fires coming from the next street. An incendiary bomb had been dropped and was causing a number of fires. The firemen were never far away and while they were working on the fires another explosion was heard and fresh fires started to emerge. It did not take long for my father to get back inside and join the family all huddled in the shelter, then another explosion, which apparently put the reservoir completely out of commission.

The next morning we ventured out to see how much damage had been done around us. In the neighbouring streets a few houses had been hit, plus quite extensive burns to houses hit by incendiary bombs. A school friend's house had been hit but the family were safe and had only minor injuries. A number of shops had been hit causing quite a bit of damage and chaos. People had suffered various injuries, but no loss of life, thank the Lord, he must have been watching over us as no bombs were dropped in our street.

Grandpa missed out on his bread and milk that night..... I don't think he missed it as his attention would have been taken up wondering where the next bomb was going to land! Even though we never undressed at night, we did have a change of clothes in the morning and went about our daily duties. I went to the local school every day, the playground was always available at recess times, but very few students were out playing. We were all a bit weary! We did have an air raid shelter erected underground, which was used of course when we had daylight raids, and these raids did increase as the months went by.

My father who was a tailor by trade, had to give his trade away during the war and work in a munitions factory. He was pretty clever actually; he made most of my sister's and my clothes.

My father was a passenger in the first liner that was torpedoed the same day as war was declared, 3rd of September 1939. He used to travel to America twice a year on business. The Americans liked English tailoring and he used to come back with a stack of orders. He survived the sinking of the ship which was called the S.S.

Athenia, but he never talked about it very much. I did some research myself and found out quite a bit about it. The U boat, a German submarine, was already in the Irish Sea when the Athenia was spotted, and as war with Germany had begun they (Germans) decided to sink the ship there and then. My father never really got over it and died when he was only 62yrs old.

Even though the actual blitz officially ended in May 1941, there were still bombs being dropped in various locations over Britain for the next couple of years or so.

When I was 14yrs old I went to a typing and shorthand school, becoming what was known as a Stenographer. I then went into an office job aged between 15 and 16yrs. Sometimes in the summer I would cycle to work, taking a short cut through what was before the war a racecourse, but during the war became a camp for American soldiers. I used to get whistled at by the soldiers, they would whistle at anybody, but anyway it gave me a bit of a boost! I remember one day at work an unexploded bomb went off not far from where I worked, I was told that an American soldier was beheaded..... not very good times to be living in!

When the war came to an end in 1945, my thoughts turned to travel. I started planning in my mind when I would be able to give it a go, so to speak. It was not long after the war was over that migration schemes were being organized by the government. I became interested in Australia and contacted Australia House in London for details. I had to be sponsored by someone who was living in Australia, and as luck would have it my sister who was a secretary to a company in London had connections in Australia and they managed to arrange a sponsorship for me. This actually came to pass in 1949 when I was 20yrs old.

My father came with me to Tilbury Dock where I boarded a ship bound for the land of Oz! By today's standard of cruise ships the S.S. Chitral was more of a barge! However, the time spent on board I thought was terrific….. a 4.5 week holiday! Even though I was travelling alone, I soon made friends on board…… a good time was held by all! Of course I missed my mother, father and sister, but the voyage soon made up for that as we went ashore at every port..... never a dull moment!

Coming to Australia under the migration scheme only cost me $10.00! I did return to England in 1951 as I was involved with someone in England with whom I became very fond of over the time I was in Australia. This person, John by name, was a civil engineer and travelled to different parts of the world. To cut a long story short, I joined him in British North Borneo a few months later. We had a house quite close to the South China Sea and I spent much of my time on the beach. In 1953 I gave birth to Dave and we were there (the name of the town was Seria) for another year, until John's contract terminated. The town of Seria is still there today, apparently, and the hospital in the neighbouring village called Kuala Lumpur is still there today. I don't think it can be called a village today as it has grown somewhat in size, plus there would have been vast changes to the hospital.

When we returned to England my life became a bit sordid. We bought a unit (John was not interested in buying a house) but after a few months John became restless and seemed to find it hard to settle down. He applied for another contract and this time it was in West Africa. Apparently there were no married quarters at that time, so Dave and I had to stay in England. No married quarters ever materialized.

The same thing happened again, but this time I felt I could not face another year on my own as I don't think he was eager to get married quarters. We arranged for the sale of the unit, and then I booked my passage back to Australia. I somehow knew he would not follow me out to Australia once his contract finished. I was on the edge of a nervous breakdown, and could not get out of England quick enough. Dave suffered the consequences of my decision to leave him behind….. for some reason which to this day I have never been able to fathom. John would not allow me to bring Dave to Australia, heaven knows why as he was never really attached to his son. This all happened in 1956, Dave was only 3yrs old when his father arranged for him to go to a boarding school (so called) in the U.K.

It was 7 years before I managed to get custody of Dave, and he arrived here in Australia in 1963, a pretty scared, disillusioned little boy. I will mention here that I returned to the U.K. in 1962 when my father was dying. After my father died my mother sold the house and came back with me to Australia. I had a lot of making up to do to Dave after those 7 years. It took a while, but slowly he came to look upon me as his mother. We have been firm friends ever since. Dave has done well paying off the mortgage on his home and becoming a naturalized Aussie! John divorced me in the U.K. and went his own merry way! I thought that perhaps I would marry an Aussie, but no, I met and married a

Scotsman, Bob….. such a good hearted placid man! Dave looked upon him as his father. Bob was very good to Dave and looked upon him as his son. I have 3 terrific sons, Dave, Paul and Brett. I think you all know that! And from these boys I have a large extended family.

Writing this I am now 93 years old, and just wish I had taken the time to stop and think where my life was going years ago. I was too busy trying to keep up with what I thought life was all about….. going to work, coming home, doing the household chores, picking up the kids…..phew!

Yes these things are part of life, but they have to be put into perspective, I went "overboard" and would drag the vacuum cleaner out of the cupboard and definitely think cleaning the carpet was more important than cooking a meal! My sons Paul & Brett well remember how obsessed I was with this housework problem!! I was a stressful person and really only felt at ease when I thought everything was clean, neat and tidy. I admit now, I missed out on being the proper mother and wife I should have been.

As the years went by I came to realise how empty my life was, and did not know how it would feel to be happy, true I did believe in God and I belonged to the Apostolic Church where Paul, Brett & myself attended every Sunday, and yes I found solace there, but once I returned home to the familiar environment, the feeling of being "bound" returned.

I firmly believe that God, or the Universe (which is widely used now, as God is anywhere and everywhere) slowly managed to change my obsession in that the way I was living was absolutely futile and would ultimately lead me to total despair. I began to see that all my energy was being sucked out of me, spending so much time on bricks & mortar, so to speak, putting so much importance on material things, achieving nothing except for anxiety and stress.

One thing that I have just remembered, my eldest son Dave (from my first marriage to John) is 14 years older than Paul & Brett, he joined the army when he was in his teens.... no doubt to get away from me and my obsessions.... but came home on leave which happened to be my birthday. I was in bed (nothing unusual for me, just another way of escaping) and he almost yanked me out of bed, saying "Come on Mum, we're going to celebrate your birthday"..... bless him. He made me put something nice on, and took me to the local hotel where we had a few drinks and a meal.

Mixing with people who seemed to be comparatively happy really helped me to realise that perhaps life was not so bad after all. I began to pull myself together and slowly I managed to direct my life onto a completely new path. My second husband Bob, who passed away at age 95 in 2017, noticed the change in me, and we began a new life together. I might add, during those dark years Bob always stood by me, he had every right to leave me but didn't. He was not a big man, but he had such a big heart! That heart has carried forward into my son's, Dave, Paul & Brett, and their extended families.....

Dave has 3 beautiful children, who between them have 5 beautiful children, Paul has 2 beautiful children, and Brett has 2 beautiful children. So in all I have 3 children, 7 grandchildren and 5 great grandchildren, and I'm sure Paul & Brett's children will flourish and continue the extended family. I see Bob in all of the family, having a laugh, a beer (or Port), calm and heart felt. He certainly was my rock.

Over the past years I have done quite a bit of study on anxiety, stress and the various struggles of life which so many of us go through. It has been an "eye-opener" for me and I long to be able to help those who are going through these trials & tribulations. To begin with there are 4 attributes which are first and foremost in these studies: Love, Peace, Joy and Gratitude.

We are all created in God's image.... Love is God – God is Love. We have all been given our share of love, unconditional love. It is up to us to portray this love in everything that we do in this life. Sometimes through circumstances it is hard to show love. Love is a most powerful "tool". No matter how rocky the journey through life is, if love manages to come to the surface, then the going becomes far smoother. Things fall into place..... challenges become less daunting. Some challenges are inevitable…. without them we would not obtain wisdom, intuition, "hands-on" experience. Peace brings inner happiness….. when the mind is in turmoil the subconscious mind is unable to connect with our soul.

When we experience true peace, we are able to connect and listen to our soul. Joy displays absolute harmony and transcends beautiful vibes. Gratitude is extremely important….. we should not take everything for granted. Be grateful for the air we breathe, for having a roof over one's head, having our needs met each day. If we show gratitude for everything we have, then the Universe is willing to give us more than we can ask or think about. My son Paul has self-published a book called 'True

Path by Paul Colquhoun (can be found on most book sites including Amazon), which reiterates the importance of connecting and listening to soul, and allowing the Universe (God/Source) to supply us with whatever we put our focus on.

~ 4 ~

# CREATE YOUR DESTINY

There is only one person that can turn your life around, to step into that doorway where you are not just existing but truly, in every area, living the life you were destined to live..... that is YOU..... waking up every morning feeling zealous about getting out of bed, ready to meet any challenge that comes your way.

Each one of us were born to live in

abundance, there is a Universal Law which connects every one of us….. spiritually, emotionally, and in health and wealth. To make sense of it all, we must "de-clutter" our minds of all the rubbish that so easily accumulates with the problems that occur with everyday living. I can hear my husband saying to me "you worry about tomorrow….. the day that never comes"! How true that statement is.

When we take the time to reflect and perhaps do a bit of day dreaming, we are able to let go of the thoughts that keep us bound to a life of negativity. Our subconscious minds can only work on the thoughts that our conscious minds produce….. if we are able to see a light at the end of every tunnel then we are heading in the right direction, and giving our subconscious minds a chance to build upon our optimistic outlook.

We are on a journey of self discovery, when we are on the wrong wave length and tuned into the wrong frequency we feel out of harmony and discouraged..... we are not connected to our spiritual DNA, so the thing to do is tune into the right frequency, tune into your true destiny. We are spiritual beings encased in a body, our bodies are made up of energy and vibrations, when we burden ourselves with problems our energy and vibrational state becomes out of balance so to speak, leaving us feeling tired and listless.

During our lifetime, we face many challenges..... these are inevitable, but we must meet them head on, so to speak, they make us more resilient, we gain wisdom from them, making us and our intuition (which we are all equipped with) much stronger. As far as money is concerned, most of us go to work every day in order to pay the bills, keep a roof over our heads and food on the table. This leaves little time for reflection and to perhaps daydream. If we can get the chance to "let go" for a while, this gives our subconscious the opportunity to clear out those thoughts that are no longer beneficial to us. Negative thoughts can cause so much unhappiness in one's life, emotionally, spiritually and physically. As I related at the beginning of this article, if there are no positive thoughts in one's mind and if living just becomes an existence, then there is nothing to look forward to..... I can certainly testify to that. When I went through that dark tunnel I could see no light at the end, and I just longed to escape by shutting myself off from the world..... I was absolutely blind to see what the world had to offer, what life was all about..... just an abyss as far as I was concerned.

I was suicidal..... I did take an overdose, even then God was watching over me. I still remember, the phone rang at that precise time and a minister from the church I belonged to knew there was something really wrong..... I managed to say that I had taken quite a few tablets and he came round straight away. To make a long story short, I remember being in Emergency for a few hours, then sent home. I will say here, that God or the Universe never abandons us. That episode was a bit scary, and I realised then perhaps life was worth living after all.

I have just done a 7-day course of Wealth Hypnosis..... I am a firm believer in hypnosis as it gets rid of "rubbish" that accumulates in the mind, and so giving the subconscious a clear path of positive thinking, optimism, being happy and grateful for all things..... and not forgetting the simple things like the air we breathe which gives us life. Getting caught up in the daily routine of everyday life, it is sometimes hard to hear that still, small voice, our soul, giving us the advice and adjustments we need from time to time. Even though I am 90, I still have dreams that I wish to fulfil, and goals that I wish to achieve before leaving this planet, but to do this I need to be wealthier. I have become receptive to the question of money..... I think of myself as becoming wealthy. To do this, think how you feel about yourself..... loving yourself is first and foremost, moving deeper into yourself. As I flow with life, financial abundance will flow to me. The Universe is full of abundance, and we are all children of the Universe, so we are also abundant. Let the images become sharper in your conscience mind, become more and more comfortable with the feeling of becoming wealthy..... what you would do when you become wealthy, make that feeling more intense, get that feeling of affluence now, don't wait until you actually have plenty of money. "When I go within myself, I will never go without". As I have said previously, there is so much potential in all of us from the day we were born, it just needs to be opened up to flow like the rivers that flow to the sea…..Never Ending!

Perhaps something I have said in this article has touched a nerve, so to speak. My name is Mary, and if you would like to contact me at all, this is my email address -

mjcluckie@gmail.com

God Bless & thank you for reading my story…….

Printed by Libri Plureos GmbH in Hamburg, Germany